THE GREAT PLAGUE!

London, 1665–1666

by Tim Cooke

Minneapolis, Minnesota

Picture Credits: Front Cover, ©Heritage Images/Topfoto; 1, ©Wellcome Collection/Look and Learn; 3, ©Wellcome Collection/Look and Learn; 5, ©Carlos Aranguiz/Shutterstock; 6–7, ©Wenceslas Hollar Digital Collection/Thomas Fisher Rare Book Library/Public Domain; 8, Deutsche Fotothek/Public Domain; 9, ©Nerthuz/Shutterstock; 10, ©IgorZh/Shutterstock; 11, ©Pictorial Press Ltd/Alamy; 12–13, ©Science History Images/Alamy; 14, ©Lance Bellers/Shutterstock; 15, ©Wellcome Collection; 16, ©Wellcome Collection/Look and Learn; 17, ©Wellcome Collection; 18, © Keith Lance/iStock; 19, ©Edward Haylan/Shutterstock; 20, ©Public Domain ; 21, ©Natalia Bulatova/Shutterstock; 22, ©The Granger Collection/Alamy; 23, ©Alastair Wallace/Shutterstock; 24, ©Lucky Team Studio/Shutterstock; 25, ©The Picture Art Collection/Alamy; 26, ©CBW/Alamy; 27, ©North Wind Picture Archives/Alamy; 28, ©Museum of London/Public Domain; 29, ©Ablakok/Public Domain.

Bearport Publishing Company Product Development Team
President: Jen Jenson; Director of Product Development: Spencer Brinker; Senior Editor: Allison Juda; Editor: Charly Haley; Associate Editor: Naomi Reich; Senior Designer: Colin O'Dea; Associate Designer: Elena Klinkner; Product Development Assistant: Anita Stasson

Brown Bear Books
Children's Publisher: Anne O'Daly; Design Manager: Keith Davis;
Picture Manager: Sophie Mortimer

Library of Congress Cataloging-in-Publication Data is available at www.loc.gov or upon request from the publisher.

ISBN: 979-8-88509-085-8 (hardcover)
ISBN: 979-8-88509-092-6 (paperback)
ISBN: 979-8-88509-099-5 (ebook)

© 2023 Brown Bear Books
This edition is published by arrangement with Brown Bear Books.

North American adaptations © 2023 Bearport Publishing Company. All rights reserved. No part of this publication may be reproduced in whole or in part, stored in any retrieval system, or transmitted in any form or by any means, electronic, mechanical, photocopying, recording, or otherwise, without written permission from the publisher.

For more information, write to Bearport Publishing, 5357 Penn Avenue South, Minneapolis, MN 55419.

CONTENTS

A Deadly Disease 4
The First Signs of Trouble 6
Disaster Strikes 12
Life or Death 20
What Happened Next 26

Key Dates 30
Quiz 30
Glossary 31
Index 32
Read More 32
Learn More Online 32

A DEADLY DISEASE

In 1665, a terrible disease tore through London, England. Almost one in every four people died of the **plague**.

Plagues were not new. In the 1300s, a plague called the Black Death swept across Europe. In a few years, it killed a third of all Europeans. There was no cure for this very **contagious** disease. The sickness most likely started in Asia and traveled to Europe by infecting people along a network of trade routes. In 1625, another outbreak of plague killed 40,000 Londoners.

Spread by Rats

We now know these plagues were caused by a **bacteria** found on fleas. It spread so quickly because fleas live on rats, which were everywhere from the city's dirty streets to its cramped, **unhygienic** homes. At the time, however, people thought the disease was caused by something in the air. They tried to protect themselves by sniffing **herbs** and lighting fires.

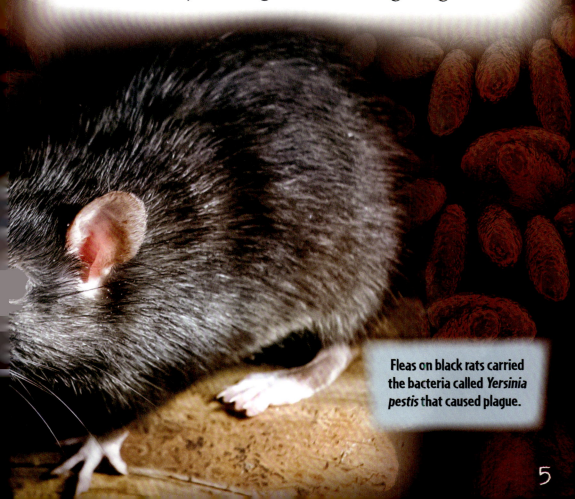

Fleas on black rats carried the bacteria called *Yersinia pestis* that caused plague.

––––––– Winter 1664–Spring 1665 –––––––

THE FIRST SIGNS OF TROUBLE

In the seventeenth century, London was the third largest city in Europe. But that would soon change.

In 1664, the main part of London was surrounded by city walls on the north bank of the Thames River. Richer citizens often lived in large houses along the river. King Charles II lived outside the city walls at Whitehall, and **Parliament** met outside the walls in Westminster. Wealthier Londoners often had relatively safe and clean places to live.

Poor Living Conditions

Meanwhile, most of the poorer people lived in **slum** neighborhoods inside narrow houses built from wood, with roofs of straw or reeds. Often, several families lived in one house, with no running water, toilets, or sewers. People emptied their waste into the streets. Rats were everywhere, but the city's feral cats usually kept their numbers under control.

Just before the plague, London had a population of about 460,000 people.

Limited Knowledge

It was common for people to die from disease in the 1600s. Doctors didn't understand much about how diseases spread or could be cured. They believed the human body contained four substances, called **humors**. Doctors said people got sick because their humors were out of balance. Illnesses could be cured by getting the humors back in balance.

The humors were thought to explain people's personalities as well as their health.

Bubonic plague spread through London. This disease attacks the **lymph system** (*in green*).

The First Signs

During the winter of 1664, people living in the poorer St. Giles neighborhood west of the city started to get sick. They got painful swellings, and their skin turned black. Along with experiencing fevers and aches, the sick often vomited uncontrollably and coughed up blood. Within a week of becoming sick, many victims died. The plague was back in London.

THREE TYPES OF PLAGUE

In addition to bubonic plague, scientists now recognize two other kinds of deadly plague. Pneumonic plague attacks the lungs. Septicemic plague affects the blood.

The Disease Spreads

In such a crowded area, fleas could easily jump from rats to humans. People who got infected could pass the infection to others before they even knew they were sick. As the first stories of the outbreak began to spread, so did fear.

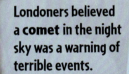

Londoners believed a **comet** in the night sky was a warning of terrible events.

A HEAVENLY SIGN?

In December 1664, a comet appeared in the night sky. **Superstitious** Londoners believed it was a sign that God was angry with them. They said the comet had been a warning.

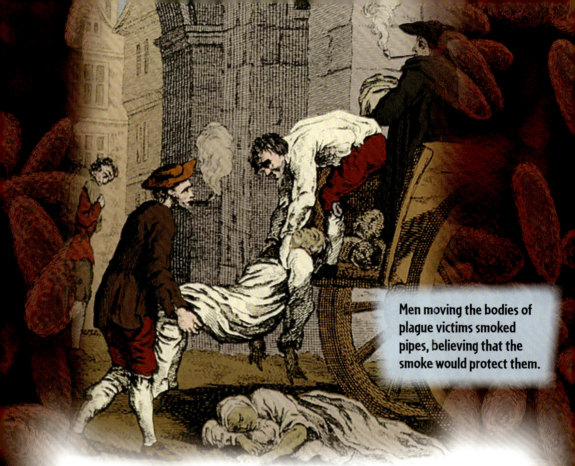

Men moving the bodies of plague victims smoked pipes, believing that the smoke would protect them.

Doomed!

By April 1665, the number of cases in St. Giles was rising quickly. Soon, the authorities ordered that if someone was sick with the plague, their whole household had to stay inside. Entire families were boarded into their homes with a message in red paint left as a warning on their front doors. Most of those kept inside homes were doomed to death, but the confinement did little to stop the spread. People started falling sick in nearby areas, too.

―― Summer 1665 ――

DISASTER STRIKES

Within just a few weeks, the numbers of dead rose dramatically as the plague spread across the city.

Although the plague was initially spread by fleas, it also passed from person to person when someone sick with plague sneezed, coughed, or breathed on others. It moved like lightning through narrow streets and overcrowded homes. People west of the city were ordered to stay indoors to stop the disease from spreading. Within the city's walls, cases were starting to rise, too.

Leaving London

Wealthy Londoners were afraid. They packed up their belongings and fled, leaving their servants behind. The streets were filled with carts heading out of the city. But poorer residents could not afford to leave. As spring turned to summer, the hot weather allowed the plague to spread even more quickly. In St. Giles alone, deaths rose from 43 in May to 17,036 in July.

Londoners who could afford to move fled from the city.

King Charles II ordered crowded theaters and other public places with crowds to close.

Who's in Charge?

King Charles II and his court left London in July, 1665, and moved 50 miles (80 km) away to the city of Oxford. The Lord Mayor of London took charge of running the city. He believed cats and dogs may have been spreading plague, so he ordered the animals to be rounded up and killed.

Out of Control

That was a terrible mistake. About 40,000 dogs and 200,000 cats were killed. As a result, the rat population exploded. With more flea-carrying rats, the plague spread even faster. By August, the death toll rose to 31,159. People were terrified. There seemed to be no way of stopping the plague. It felt as though everyone would die.

Dead bodies appeared in London's streets.

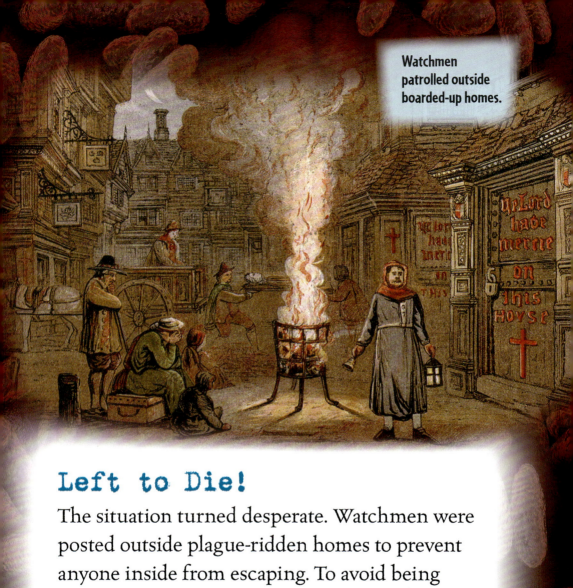

Watchmen patrolled outside boarded-up homes.

Left to Die!

The situation turned desperate. Watchmen were posted outside plague-ridden homes to prevent anyone inside from escaping. To avoid being trapped in their homes, many families tried to hide it when someone in the household was sick. They continued their normal daily lives, which only caused the disease to spread more quickly.

Lists of the Dead

Infections continued to rise. Each week between December 1664 and December 1665, plague deaths were recorded on special lists called bills of mortality. The sheets were printed and sold for a penny. People could read about which neighborhoods had the highest death rates.

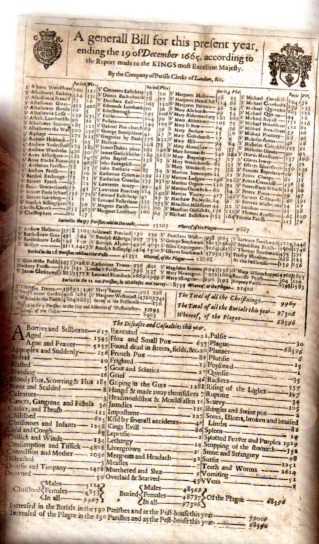

This bill of mortality reports that 68,596 people died of plague in 1665.

"Bring Out Your Dead!"

Many worried the dead bodies of the victims were still **infectious**, so they had to be taken care of quickly to prevent further spread. At night, **porters** walked through the empty streets shouting, "Bring out your dead!" They collected the dead for burial.

Bodies were usually buried at night to avoid spreading infection.

Charterhouse Square in London stands on the site of a former plague pit.

Plague Pits

Church graveyards soon filled up. When there was no more room, people began to dig huge pits in fields and other empty spaces outside the city walls. They buried hundreds of victims together in large graves. Many of these plague pits are still buried beneath the city.

UNCOVERING PLAGUE PITS

In 2021, **archaeologists** working on a new train station in London discovered a number of bodies. By studying the skeletons, they figured out that the victims had died from bubonic plague.

— Summer 1665 —

LIFE OR DEATH

As the plague spread, new science emerged. So did fake cures.

In the 1600s, some people wanted to make medicine more scientific. They tried to understand the causes of the plague by studying its **symptoms**. Still, the illness scared people. And many fake doctors started taking advantage of the citizens.

Fake plague doctors were nicknamed Doctor Beak.

People sniffed herbs, flowers, and spices to protect against the air they thought caused the plague. This did nothing to prevent the spread.

Fake Doctors

At the beginning of the plague, as many as half of London's 600 doctors had fled the city. That left plenty of space for fake doctors to start selling fake medicines. These phony doctors wore long overcoats and large, pointed masks shaped like the beak of a bird.

QUACK DOCTORS

Fake plague doctors were sometimes called quack doctors. Some think the name came from the beak masks, or because they sounded like a bunch of quacking ducks when they shouted through their masks to attract customers to buy their medicine. Today, bad doctors are sometimes still called quacks.

People who left London were often not welcome in places terrified of the plague.

Spreading Death

When those who had the means to leave did so, they took the plague with them. People were not allowed to leave unless they had an official letter that said they were healthy. However, many who left were infected but didn't yet have symptoms. Others carried fleas with plague **germs**. The disease soon spread far and wide.

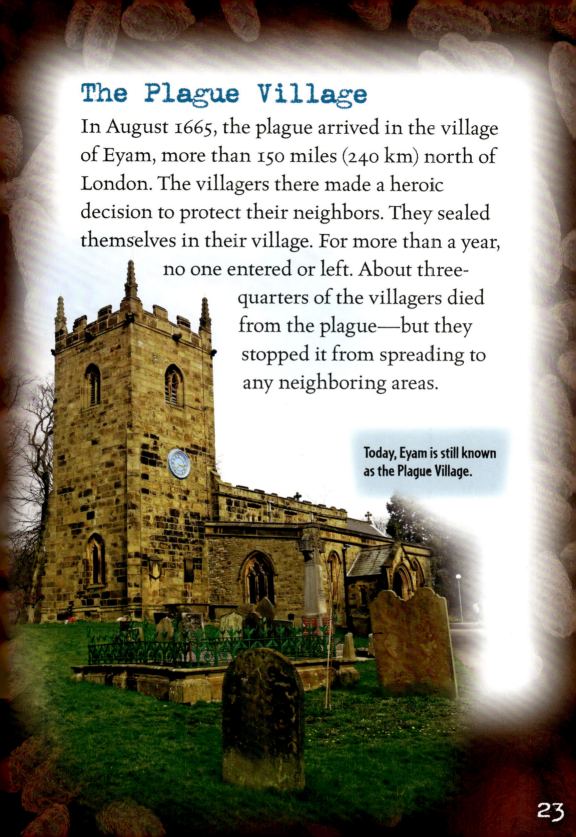

The Plague Village

In August 1665, the plague arrived in the village of Eyam, more than 150 miles (240 km) north of London. The villagers there made a heroic decision to protect their neighbors. They sealed themselves in their village. For more than a year, no one entered or left. About three-quarters of the villagers died from the plague—but they stopped it from spreading to any neighboring areas.

Today, Eyam is still known as the Plague Village.

As fall arrived and temperatures fell, so did the number of cases of plague.

Numbers Fall

The peak of plague deaths came the week of September 19, 1665, when 7,165 people died. Then, the numbers started to fall. Nobody really knows why. One theory is that as the weather grew cooler, the bacteria that caused plague died. Some think the fleas carrying plague stopped moving from rats to people. Still others believed there were far fewer people left in London to get infected.

An Empty City

By the fall, London was a very different city. Grass grew on the streets at the king's palace. Boats no longer sailed on the River Thames. Theaters, dance halls, and **taverns** stood empty. The stray dogs and cats that once roamed the streets were nowhere to be found.

Londoner Samuel Pepys described the plague in his diary.

QUOTATION FROM SAMUEL PEPYS'S DIARY

"[H]ow empty the streets are and **melancholy**. So many poor sick people in the streets full of sores; and so many sad stories overheard as I walk. Everybody talking of this dead, and that man sick, and so many in this place, and so many in that."

Early 1666
WHAT HAPPENED NEXT

In February 1666, the king returned to London, signaling that the worst of the plague had passed.

While people were still dying from the disease during the winter of 1666, it was not as many as the previous summer. As the weather grew colder and the effects of the plague lessened, more people returned to London. The streets started to fill as businesses once again opened their doors.

King Charles II ordered fires to be set in order to **purify** the air.

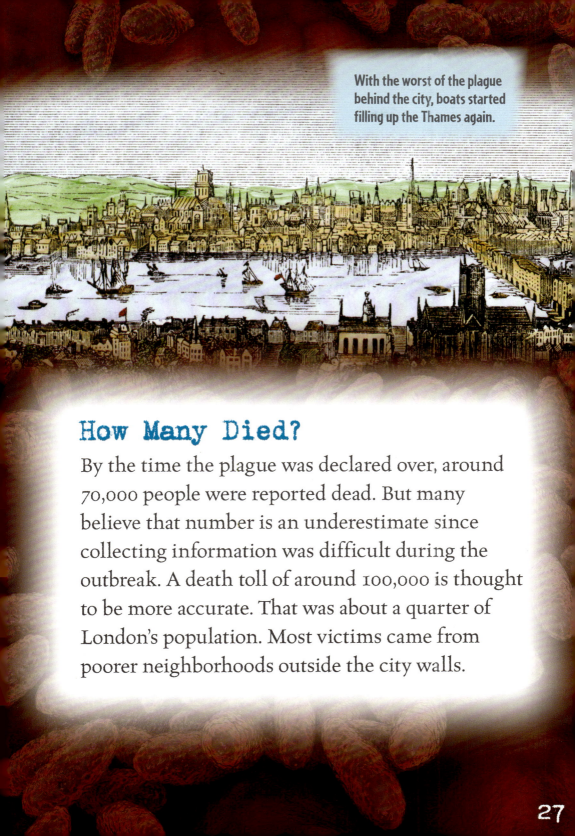

With the worst of the plague behind the city, boats started filling up the Thames again.

How Many Died?

By the time the plague was declared over, around 70,000 people were reported dead. But many believe that number is an underestimate since collecting information was difficult during the outbreak. A death toll of around 100,000 is thought to be more accurate. That was about a quarter of London's population. Most victims came from poorer neighborhoods outside the city walls.

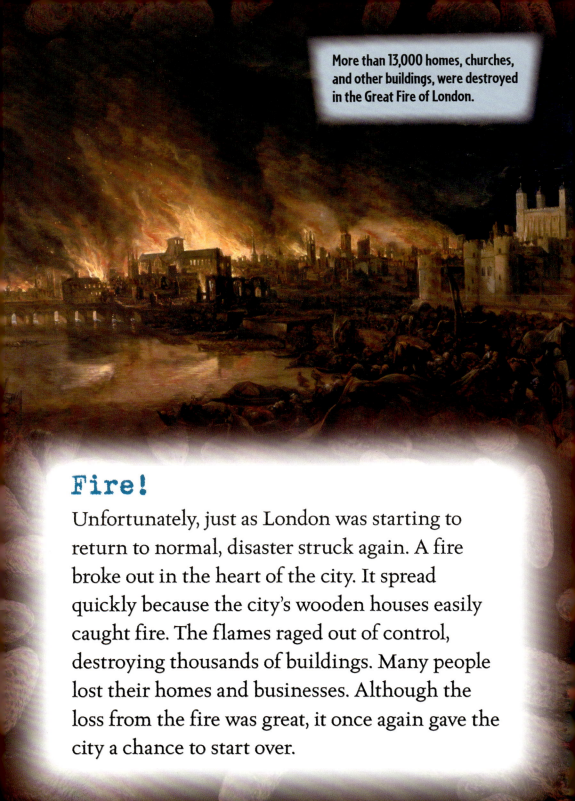

More than 13,000 homes, churches, and other buildings, were destroyed in the Great Fire of London.

Fire!

Unfortunately, just as London was starting to return to normal, disaster struck again. A fire broke out in the heart of the city. It spread quickly because the city's wooden houses easily caught fire. The flames raged out of control, destroying thousands of buildings. Many people lost their homes and businesses. Although the loss from the fire was great, it once again gave the city a chance to start over.

A New City

The fire killed many of London's rats. As the people of London began to rebuild, they made the streets wider and lined them with sidewalks. All new houses were built from stone or brick to reduce the risk of another fire. And a new kind of sewers made London cleaner and healthier. London was on its way to becoming a modern city. It never faced another outbreak of plague.

The rebuilding of London sparked important changes in the city.

KEY DATES

1664
Winter Rumors spread of the first plague cases in St. Giles

1665
May There are 43 confirmed victims

June Certificate of health are needed to travel from town to town

July The king leaves London

The Lord Mayor orders all cats and dogs to be killed

August Large pits are dug to bury plague victims

The plague reaches Eyam

September Deaths peak at over 7,000 a week

November The number of weekly deaths starts to fall

1666
February King Charles II returns to London

September The Great Fire of London destroys much of the city

QUIZ

How much have you learned about the plague in London? It's time to test your knowledge! Then, check your answers on page 32.

1. **What did Londoners see as a warning sign in December 1664?**
   a) a black ship sailing up the River Thames
   b) a comet shooting through the night sky
   c) Buildings on fire

2. **Where was the first recorded case of the plague?**
   a) in Westminster
   b) in Oxford
   c) in St. Giles

3. **How did the village of Eyam stop plague?**
   a) they listened to quack doctors
   b) they closed off the city
   c) they killed all the dogs

4. **What happened to London's cats at the start of the plague?**
   a) they all ran away
   b) they were killed
   c) the Lord Mayor adopted them

5. **Which month did the plague peak in London?**
   a) July
   b) August
   c) September

GLOSSARY

archaeologists people who study the past by digging up old physical objects

bacteria tiny, microscopic organisms that cause disease

comet a ball of dust and ice in space that is visible on Earth

contagious passing easily from person to person

germs tiny living organisms that can cause disease

herbs plants that are used in medicines and while cooking

humors four substances that were believed to determine the state of a person's health in the Middle Ages

infectious able to pass on a disease

lymph system a part of the immune system that protects the body from disease

melancholy sad or depressed

parliament a British lawmaking body of government

plague a disease that causes death and spreads quickly to a large number of people

porters officers in London whose job was to keep an eye on the residents of the city

purify to make something clean

slum a poor neighborhood with low-quality housing

superstitious believing that events and signs influence good or bad luck

symptoms the physical signs of a sickness

taverns places where people could buy food and drinks

unhygienic unclean and likely to cause sickness

INDEX

Bills of Mortality 17
Black Death 4
cats 7, 14–15, 25, 30
Charles II, King 6, 14, 26, 30
comet 10, 30
doctors 8, 20–21
Eyam 23, 30
fleas 4–5, 10, 12, 15, 22–24, 30
Great Fire of London, the 28–30
humors 8
Lord Mayor 14, 30
Parliament 6, 30
Pepys, Samuel 25
plague pits 19, 30
rats 4–5, 7, 10, 15, 24, 29
St. Giles 9–11, 13, 30
St. Paul's 28–29
Thames, River 6, 25–27, 30
theaters 14, 25
Westminster 6, 30
Whitehall 6, 25

READ MORE

Loh-Hagan, Virginia. *The Plague (Surviving History)*. Ann Arbor, MI: Cherry Lake, 2021.

Messner, Kate. *Plagues and Pandemics (History Smashers)*. New York: Random House, 2021.

Torres, John A. *Petrifying Plagues (Creepy, Kooky Science)*. New York: Enslow Publishing, 2020.

LEARN MORE ONLINE

1. Go to **www.factsurfer.com** or scan the QR code below
2. Enter **"Great Plague"** into the search box.
3. Click on the cover of this book to see a list of websites.

Answers to the quiz on page 30

Answers: 1) B; 2) C; 3) B; 4) B; 5) C